W9-DIS-386

SPECTRUM® READERS

LEVEL 1

BUSY! Insects

By Lisa Kurkov

Carson-Dellosa Publishing

SPECTRUM®
An imprint of Carson-Dellosa Publishing, LLC
P.O. Box 35665
Greensboro, NC 27425-5665

© 2014, Carson-Dellosa Publishing, LLC. Except as permitted under the United States Copyright Act, no part of this publication may be reproduced, stored, or distributed in any form or by any means (mechanically, electronically, recording, etc.) without the prior written consent of Carson-Dellosa Publishing, LLC. Spectrum is an imprint of Carson-Dellosa Publishing, LLC.

carsondellosa.com

Printed in the USA. All rights reserved.
ISBN 978-1-4838-0114-8

01-002141120

Insects have six legs.
They hatch from eggs.
Their bodies have three parts.
They have no backbones.
Busy insects are everywhere!

Cicada

Busy cicadas make a loud humming noise. Some can be heard a mile away!

Mosquito

Busy mosquitoes feed on blood.
They leave behind an itchy, red bump.

Leaf Mantis

Busy leaf mantises hide on plants. Predators will not spot them.

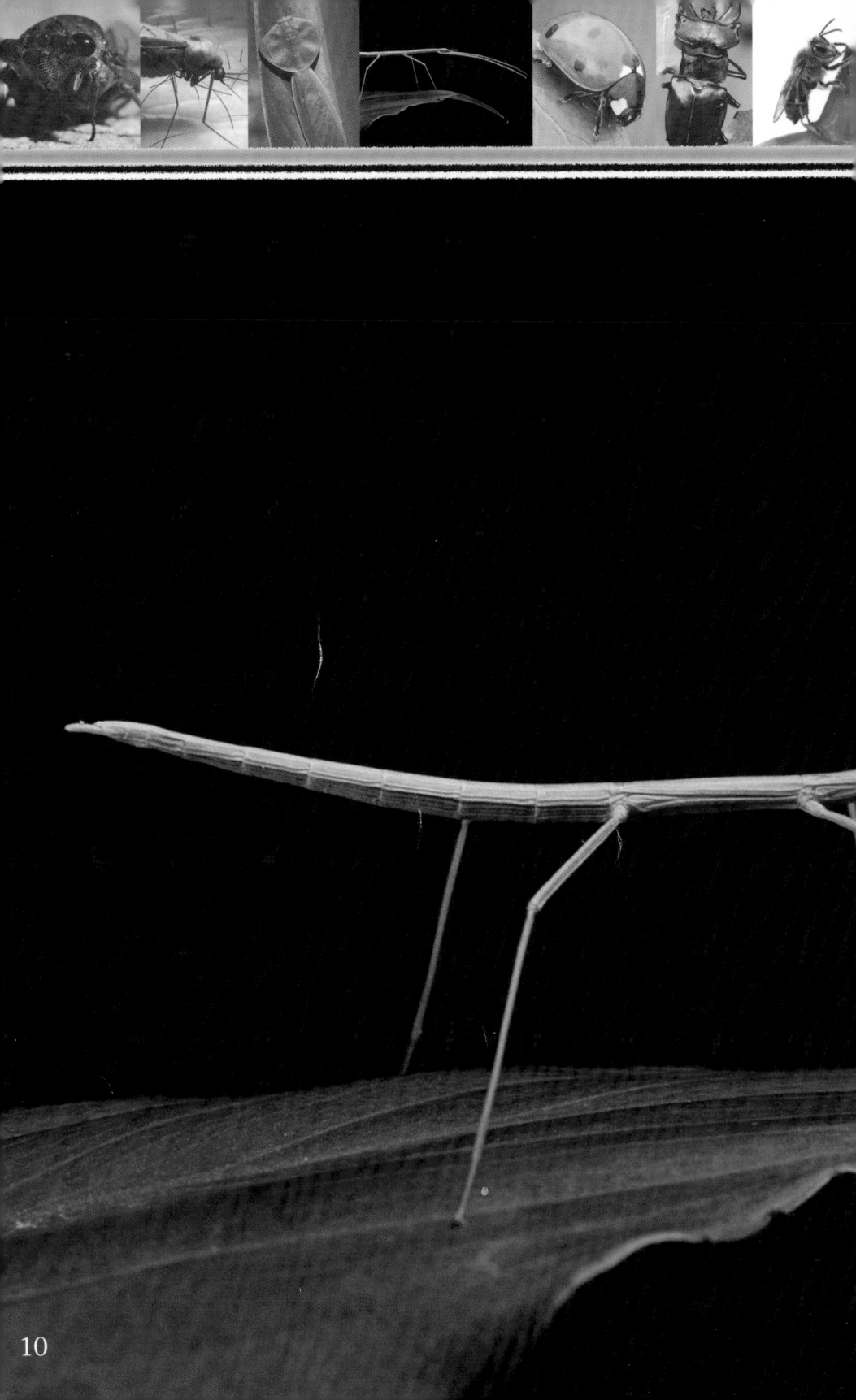

Stick Insect

Busy stick insects pretend to be twigs. One kind is almost two feet long!

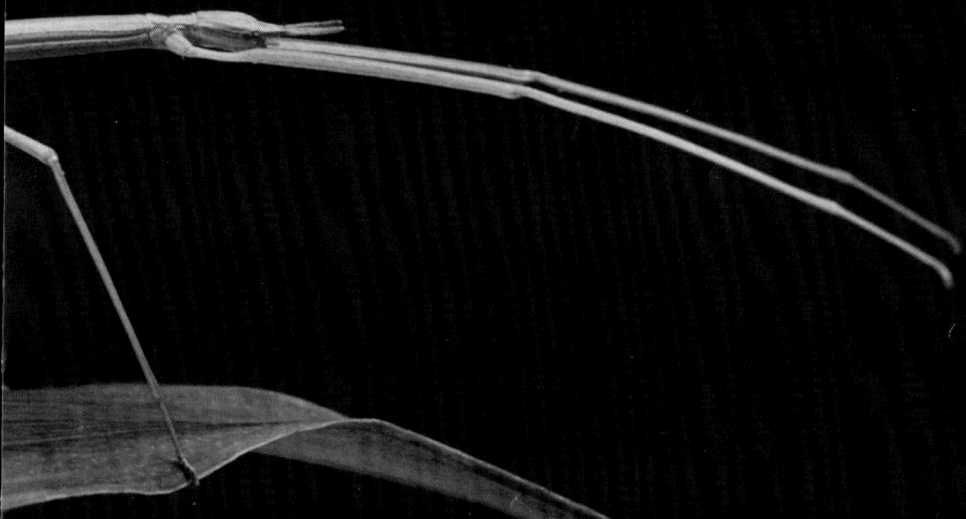

Ladybug

Busy ladybugs eat insects that harm plants. They help protect plants in a farmer's field.

Stag Beetle

Busy stag beetles use their jaws to fight. Their big jaws look like antlers.

Bee

Busy bees carry pollen from flower to flower. They help fruits and vegetables grow.

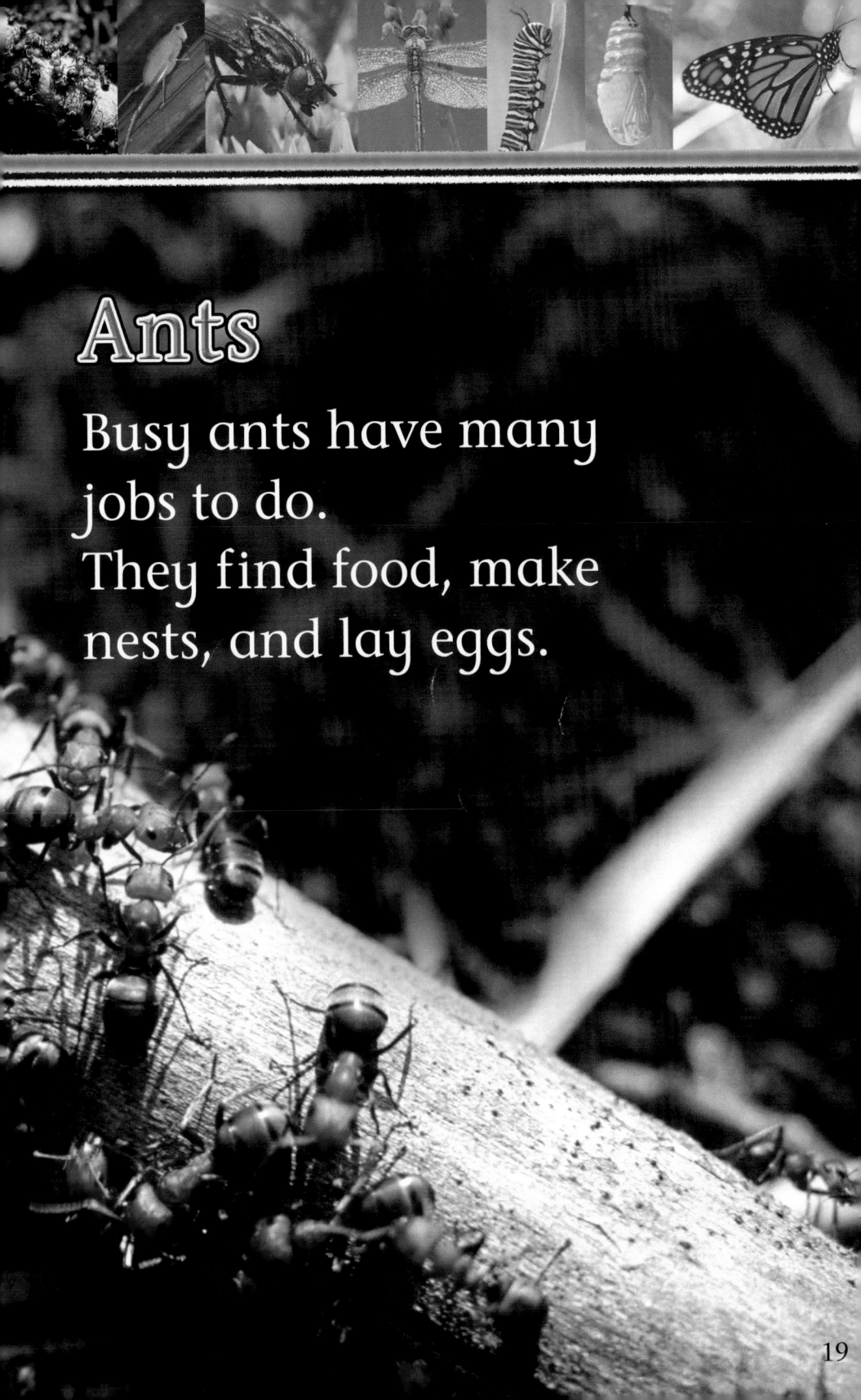

Ants

Busy ants have many jobs to do.
They find food, make nests, and lay eggs.

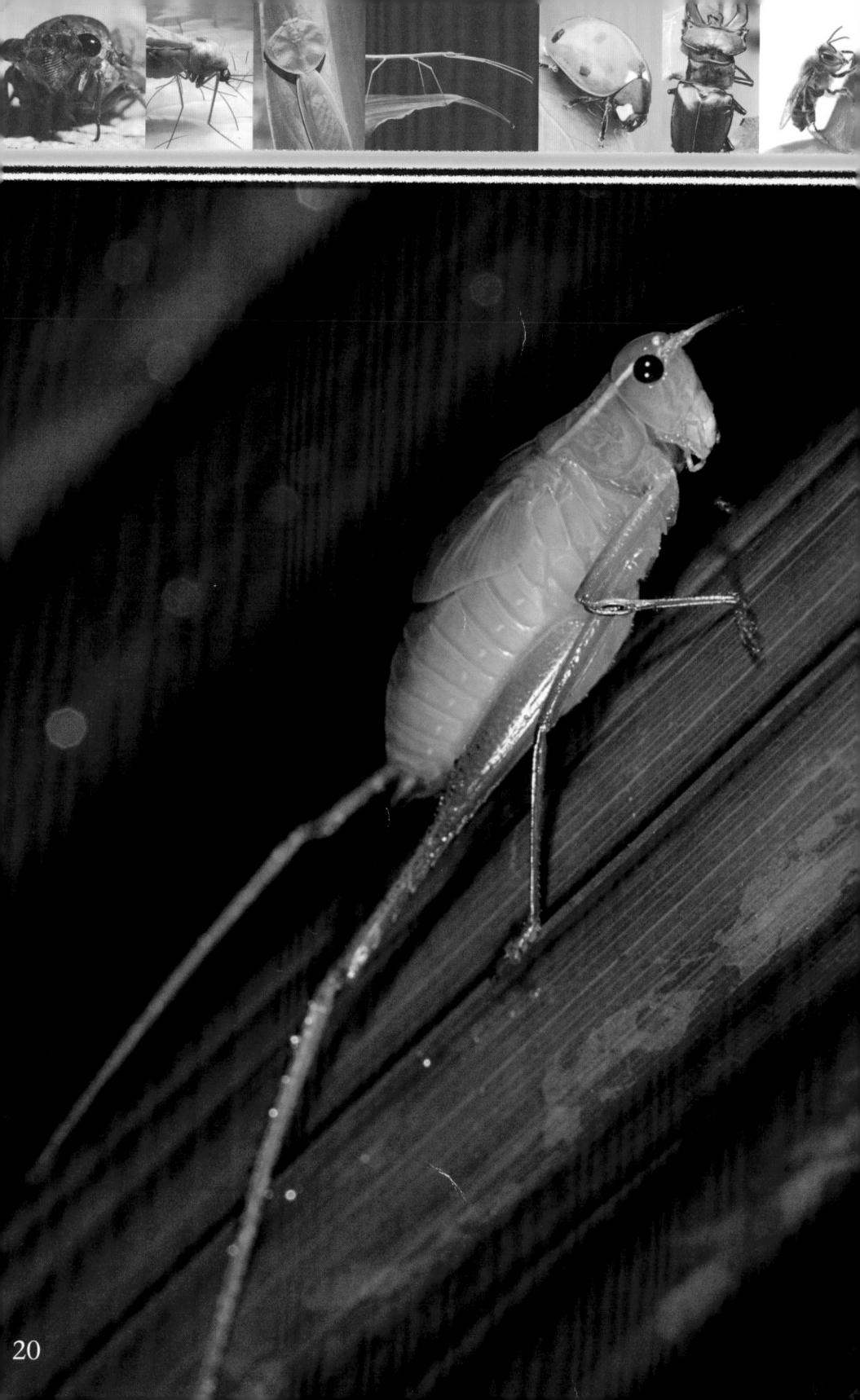

Grasshopper

Busy grasshoppers jump in the grass.
Some can leap almost two feet!

Fly

Busy flies search for food
outside and inside.
They use their feet to taste!

Dragonfly

Busy dragonflies hover over ponds and streams. They can fly backward like helicopters!

Monarch Caterpillar

Busy caterpillars munch leaves. They store energy to get ready for a big change.

Monarch Chrysalis

Busy chrysalises (KRIS uh lis ses) have wiggly caterpillars inside. Soon, a butterfly will emerge.

Monarch Butterfly

Busy monarch butterflies fly long distances. In the fall, they travel to Mexico!

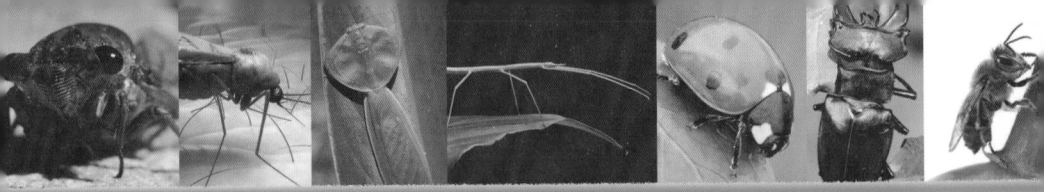

BUSY! Insects Comprehension Questions

1. What are three things insects have in common?
2. What do mosquitoes eat?
3. What helps a leaf mantis and stick insect hide?
4. How do ladybugs help people?
5. How does a stag beetle use its jaws?
6. Why are bees so important?
7. Where do dragonflies live?
8. How far can a grasshopper jump?
9. What part of its body does a fly use to taste?
10. What is a chrysalis?
11. Where do monarchs go when it gets cold outside?